Celtic Key Patterns

Z figure with three two-diagonal
triangles, Inchcolm, Fife.

Iain Bain

celtic
key patterns

Constable · London

First published in Great Britain 1993
by Constable and Company Limited
3 The Lanchesters, 162 Fulham Palace Road
London W6 9ER
Copyright © 1993 Iain Bain
The right of Iain Bain to be identified as
the author of this work has been asserted by
him in accordance with the Copyright, Designs
and Patents Act 1988

ISBN 0 09 470690 5 (hardback)
ISBN 0 09 471820 2 (paperback)

Set in Monophoto Helvetica Nominal by
Service Filmsetting Ltd, Manchester
Printed in Great Britain by
BAS Printers Ltd, Over Wallop

A CIP catalogue record for this book is
available from the British Library

Contents

Illustrations   vi

Acknowledgements   vii

Preface   viii

Introduction   ix

Chapter 1
An introduction to Z patterns   1

Chapter 2
Zed or Z patterns   3

Chapter 3
Z patterns with internal variations   11

Chapter 4
W patterns   26

Chapter 5
Hook patterns   33

Chapter 6
Small patterns   41

Chapter 7
Panel shapes, treatments and embellishments   48

Chapter 8
Diagonal setting-out   52

Appendix: extract from *Early Christian Monuments* by J. Romilly Allen   63

Index   87

Illustrations

Colour plates: Facing page

Plate 1. Folio 17b from the *Lindisfarne Gospels*   16
reproduced by permission of the British Library

Plate 2. Folio 95 from the *Lindisfarne Gospels*   17
reproduced by permission of the British Library

Plate 3. Folio 210b from the *Lindisfarne Gospels*   32
reproduced by permission of the British Library

Plate 4. Folio 1v from the *Book of Kells*   33
reproduced by permission of the Board of Trinity College, Dublin

Plate 5. Folio 2v from the *Book of Kells*   48
reproduced by permission of the Board of Trinity College, Dublin

Plate 6. Folio 202v from the *Book of Kells*   49
reproduced by permission of the Board of Trinity College, Dublin

Plate 7. Folio 290v from the *Book of Kells*   64
reproduced by permission of the Board of Trinity College, Dublin

Plate 8. Folio 291v from the *Book of Kells*   65
reproduced by permission of the Board of Trinity College, Dublin

Black and white photographs: Page

Z figure, Inchcolm, Fife   Frontispiece
reproduced by permission of the National Museums of Scotland

Carved stone at Rosemarkie, Ross-shire   xi
from *Early Christian Monuments* by J. Romilly Allen

St Donnans, Eigg, Inner Hebrides   8
reproduced by permission of the National Museums of Scotland

Rosemarkie No 1, Easter Ross   10
reproduced by permission of the National Monuments Record of Scotland

The St Andrews Stone, Fife   17
photograph T. E. Gray, Edinburgh

Single triangle pattern, Invergowrie, Angus   27
reproduced by permission of the National Museums of Scotland

Small triangle, Invergowrie, Angus   42
reproduced by permission of the National Museums of Scotland

Doubled key pattern Z figure, Jedburgh, Roxburghshire   51
reproduced by permission of the National Museums of Scotland

Acknowledgements

For their helpfulness and courtesy on my visits to their Museum and selection of photographs, my thanks go to National Museums of Scotland, Queen Street, Edinburgh.

For their helpfulness and courtesy in the provision of photographs of the Rosemarkie stone and the St. Andrews stone No. 14, my thanks go to Historic Scotland, Edinburgh, in particular to J.W. White, and to T.E. Gray of Edinburgh who provided the St. Andrews stone photograph.

My thanks also go to Historic Scotland in the names of David Eaton and Mrs. Eileen Eaton, the custodians of St. Andrews Cathedral and Meigle museums, for their helpfulness and courtesy over several years on visits to these museums, and I am grateful also to David Eaton for bringing to my attention the existence of the Historic Scotland museum.

For tracing in ink most of my pencilled key pattern drawings my thanks go to Anne Bowyer, one of the earliest of my 'Celtic knotwork' readers.

For their patience and understanding during the research and preparation of the book my grateful thanks go to my wife Nora and family and friends.

Lastly my thanks go to Constable, in particular Richard Tomkins, for their help, understanding and patience throughout. To give one example of the problems, it is easy to draw diagrams on graph paper and to trace these on to transparent paper, but moisture content affects all types of paper, and exact registering thereafter is difficult.

Preface

Much of the preface to *Celtic Knotwork* applies so suitably to *Celtic Key Patterns* that it is virtually repeated here. The key patterns produced by the ancients are comparatively easy to copy, but mere copying cannot unlock the mystery of their construction nor does it lead to a creative use of the art. It is my hope that these methods for the reconstruction and creation of Celtic key patterns will lead to an upsurge of interest in this fascinating subject.

In the sense that the methods cover a wide range of key patterns from the simple to the complicated, they are not elementary, yet they *are* simple enough to be within the understanding of readers of almost any age and capability. Even those who may be put off by some of the simple mathematical symbols need not despair because these can be ignored, the mind being applied principally to the formation of the 'V', 'Z', 'W' or 'Hook' figures which form the skeletons of all key patterns.

Indeed I believe, as in the case of Celtic knotwork, that this is an art form for the person who feels 'I can't draw and this is far too complicated for me'. On the contrary, the simple disciplines of the construction methods may surprise that person into an awareness of his or her unsuspected artistic ability.

The Celts developed four principal forms of ornament; knotwork, spirals, key patterns and interlacing human, beast, bird and reptile figures. Most surviving designs are on monumental stones or in illuminated manuscripts, and most contain more than one of these forms, each in its own space or panel, within the overall layout.

All forms of Celtic art have a geometric appearance, and although each has its own particular characteristics, knotwork and key patterns have some common factors, one being the 'cord' or 'path'. In knotwork I prefer the word 'cord' because knotwork consists of representations of one or more loosely knotted cords. Key patterns, on the other hand, have the appearance of angular paths which keep separating and rejoining systematically.

Another factor common to most knotwork and key patterns is the manner in which cords or paths stand out in relief, the background having been carved away in the stone carvings and painted in dark colours in the manuscripts.

As with knotwork, all key patterns have a standard form. In standard key patterns, virtually all construction lines are straight and the angle of the diagonal lines is 45 degrees. The word 'virtually' is used because occasionally curved spirals appear within a pattern.

There are two quite different types of Celtic key patterns. Each contains straight line spirals. One has single spirals, which I name 'hook' patterns because that is what they look like; the other has double, or intertwining spirals which I name 'Z' patterns because of the Z figures which appear in their construction.

The main feature of Celtic key patterns is the predominance of straight lines in their standard rendering. These lines form paths which usually create the triangular spaces which give the patterns their unique character. But there is nothing standard about the work of the ancient scribes in the illuminated manuscripts. 'Supernatural' is the only appropriate word to describe the minuteness of the detail achieved by the scribes. Good examples are in the central panel on folio 27V in the *Book of Kells*, and on folio 95 in the *Lindisfarne Gospels* (Plate 2 facing page 17).

Key patterns are remarkably easy to draw, particularly so on 2mm graph paper, which avoids the need for diagonal setting-out lines. Indeed I am reluctant to suggest this method of setting-out because of the risk that it might discourage the use of diagonal lines other than 45°.

In *Celtic Knotwork* I refer to the Victorian antiquarian J. Romilly Allen and his research into the methods of the construction of Celtic art contained in his massive book *Celtic Art in Pagan and Christian Times*, 400 copies of which were printed in 1903 by Neil & Co. of Edinburgh for the Society of Antiquaries of Scotland. In this his drawings of knotwork patterns emphasise the plait and the effect of breaking and re-joining the cords of a plait to form knotwork. As such they are diagrams only and are not intended to represent finished knotwork patterns. Unlike knotwork, however, key patterns normally are composed of straight lines which do produce finished patterns, and Romilly Allen's drawings are excellent. They should be available to the general public and are included here in an appendix.

He numbered each of his patterns, and these numbers are used for reference throughout this book. He also gave the localities of the patterns, which, as far as I am aware, are unchanged today.

In my introduction to *Celtic Knotwork*, published in 1986, I wrote that more and more people were becoming interested and involved in arts and crafts. As I write this in March 1992 in the midst of a depression, this same interest is alive and flourishing, perhaps because, in hard times, people look for ways in which to amuse and employ themselves.

In *Celtic Knotwork* I stated that I was offering no alternative construction methods for the key patterns, spirals, zoomorphics and the other forms of ornament contained in my father's book *Celtic Art, the Methods of Construction*. This was so with the new book until I found myself doodling with Celtic patterns on 2mm graph paper, which provided all of the setting-out lines needed to draw standard key patterns directly. I earnestly plead, however, that non-standard key patterns must be practised once the construction methods are understood.

Inevitably the introduction to this book could not be finalised before its production in manuscript form, and one of the problems I have encountered during my key pattern researches is a nagging doubt about the title 'Celtic'. The Lindisfarne Gospels were written in the monastery of Lindisfarne on Holy Island, Northumberland in Anglo-Saxon times. There is evidence that the Books of Kells and Durrow were written there also, and that all three were removed from Lindisfarne to escape Viking invasions.

But the wonderful ornament produced by the scribes of Lindisfarne, Kells and Durrow was not confined to illuminated manuscripts. Stone carvings with similar ornament, ranging on the east coast of Britain from Caithness in Scotland to Humberside and beyond, belong to the same Anglo-Saxon period. This huge area was the land of the Picts, which suggests that the Saxons conquered an already cultured race. No doubt the Saxons brought their own cultures, but they would certainly be influenced by exising native cultures.

On this evidence, 'Pictish' is the proper title for this wonderful art, but because of the long existing use of the world 'Celtic' it is wiser for me to avoid confusion by continuing to use the title 'Celtic'.

One important factor is the existence of Celtic stone carvings in Celtic Wales, mainly small patterns, some of which are illustrated in Chapter 6.

Carved stone No 1 at Rosemarkie, Ross-shire. Panel of symbols on back at top of slab. From *Early Christian Monuments of Scotland* by J. Romilly Allen.

Chapter 1

An introduction to Z patterns.
The half Z or V pattern.

Although squared paper is ideal for drawing Celtic key patterns, and 2mm spacing is ideal for general use, it must be emphasised that non-standard patterns should be attempted on plain paper once the basic principles are understood.

Start with a simple pattern in a rectangle six spaces wide.

Locations include St Andrews in Fife and Rosemarkie in Easter Ross.

Key patterns can be turned upside down and mirrored.

To minimise confusion, most patterns will be drawn as shown here, with the top left hand corner closed, but the other (or mirrored) aspect is equally correct and should be practised.

R.A. stands for
J. Romilly Allen.
See Appendix p. 63.

R.A. 926

1   2   3   4   Finishing treatments.

An even number of diagonals is required.

Complete each stage before starting the next. The dots emphasise the full diagonal separation of approaching lines.

The finishing treatment should be bold. Indeed there is no reason why the black lines should not be as thick or thicker than the spaces between.

The same pattern makes a border design:-

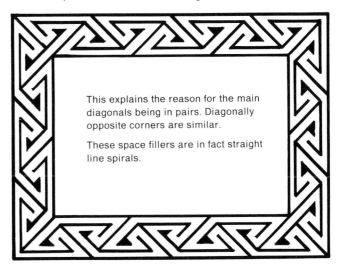

This explains the reason for the main diagonals being in pairs. Diagonally opposite corners are similar.

These space fillers are in fact straight line spirals.

Due to reduction in printing, the graph paper spacing is less than 2mm.

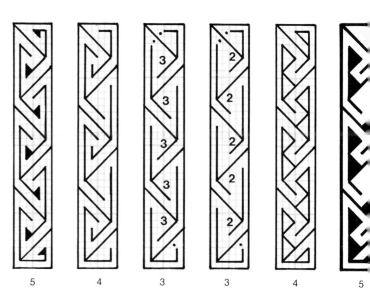

| 5 | 4 | 3 | 3 | 4 | 5 |

The previous pattern introduced tiny triangles. By reducing the short tails in stage 3 from 3 spaces to 2 spaces, pairs of larger triangles can be formed.

As the eye looks at figures 3 the black lines could suggest short single line paths, but as the patterns develop the eye also observes black lines bordering continuous white paths. This is particularly so with the introduction of the larger triangles.

These white paths have much in common with the paths in my book *Celtic Knotwork*, the main difference being the angularity of the key patterns and the smooth flowing curves of the knotwork patterns.

A common factor is the difference in width or thickness between paths running vertically or horizontally and paths running diagonally.

In key patterns this can be adjusted in the finishing treatment by working outside (in this case), or inside the vertical and horizontal lines.

This is an example of the Celts' deliberate manipulation of geometry which I describe overleaf and in *Celtic Knotwork*.

Try a border version of this larger triangle pattern. As you can see the pattern repeats in units of 12 spaces.

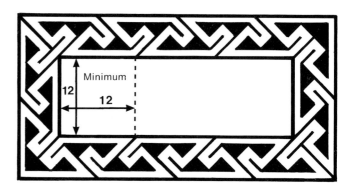

Chapter 2
Zed or Z patterns

The basic Z pattern, described by Romilly Allen as one bay wide.

This is a widened version of the V pattern, showing the full Z figure which provides the backbone for many key patterns. There are numerous examples in the illuminated manuscripts and on the Pictish stone carvings.

Particularly good examples are in the Lindisfarne Gospels on folio 17b.

Use spacer dots as before to ensure that full diagonal spacing is maintained.

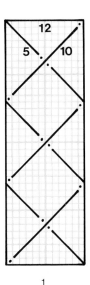

1

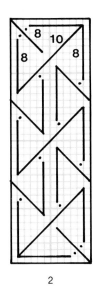

2

3

4

Figure 4 is the complete setting-out diagram. Full crosses are required in figure 1 to ensure that diagonally opposite corners are similar.

The finished design, straddling the diagonal lines and working inside or outside the vertical and horizontal path lines in the interest of constant path widths.

The Celts were masters of geometry and this is another example of their 'approximate' geometry.

The actual difference is the difference between 1.414 and 2, or 0.707 and 1, or approximately $\frac{3}{4}$ and 1.

This is similar to the $\frac{3}{4}$ rule which I refer to in *Celtic Knotwork*.

Generally throughout the book narrow border paths are used in the setting-out stages as shown here.

A 2 bay version of the Z pattern.

R.A. 974

3

4

An overall version is opposite.

Finish.

An overall version of the Z pattern.

Z figures can have different sizes and numbers of Z triangles

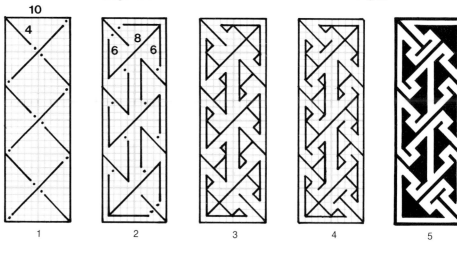

1   2   3   4   5

Two diagonal triangles △ are required to form the U turns. The outer triangle
can be smaller, △ one diagonal, or larger △ three diagonal.

1 & 2   3   4   5

Larger Z triangles are possible, as illustrated on page 28.

Z figures with 3 two-diagonal triangles. Two sources are Inchcolm, Fife (frontispiece) and Gattonside (near Melrose) in the Scottish borders.

1

2

3

4

Draw the Zs and half Zs.   Form the triangles.   Add the Z and half Z tails.

R.A. 933

5

6

Finish.

Form the extra path U turns.
A photograph is on page ii (frontispiece).

7

Another version of the previous pattern, not listed by R.A. but see opposite.

Stage 4 on the
previous page

5a

6a (Finish)

Note the short lines attached to the Z diagonals (normally kept free), which a▮
necessary to form the additional U turns.

St Donnans, Eigg, Inner Hebrides

24

22

20

Stages 1 to 4 of the previous patterns.

5b

5b Finish.

5c

5c Finish.

British Museum. Bibl. Reg., I.E. vi.

The page 7 three-triangle Z pattern but with a one-unit triangle on each leg.

14

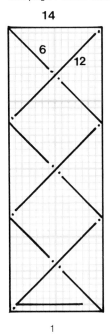

1

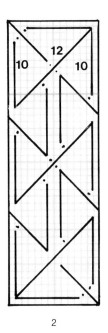

2

3

4

5

6

Rosemarkie No.1,
Easter Ross.

Chapter 3

Z patterns with internal variations.

12

By omitting the internal Z verticals, different internal arrangements are possible.

In the following examples the Z figures have attachments. The border hooks are free. Double straight-line spirals are formed.

R.A. 946

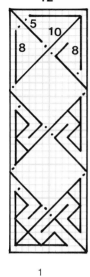

1

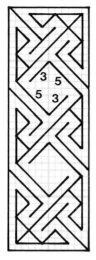

2

3

St Andrews No.14
(Edge of stone.)

As shown here, and as drawn by Romilly Allen, the internal figures represent flags.

As carved on the stone the 'flags' are not much wider than the flag posts.

As before most patterns are drawn as shown here, with the top left-hand corner closed.

R.A. 944

2a

3a

St Vigeans
Tayside No.12.
Book of Kells folio
2 V.

More double straight-line internal spirals. Again the Z figures have attachments.

12

R.A. 945

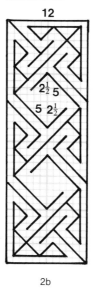  

2b   3b

See also Romilly Allen's figures Nos 960 and 961.

St Andrews, Fife, No.10.
Govan, Strathclyde, No.34
Rosemarkie No.1
Book of Kells folio 4R.

This pattern introduces circular spirals.

R.A. 947

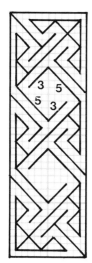   

Figure 2 on previous page

2c   3c

Book of Kells folio 18 R.

In these examples the Z figures are free. The border hooks have attachments. Again double straight-line spirals are formed.

12

R.A. 943

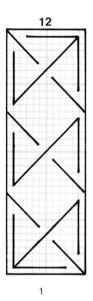

1

2

3a

4a
Burghead,
Aberdeenshire

The Norham pattern below is shown one bay wide as illustrated by Romilly Allen. It is, in fact, two bays wide.

R.A. 941

3b

4b

3c

4c

Norham, Northumberland. Hurworth, Durham. (Now at Durham Cathedral.) Kells, Ireland.
Compare this pattern with St Andrews No.14 on page 11.

This pattern is not recorded by Romilly Allen and therefore may be original.
Compare this pattern with St Andrews No.10 on page 12.

The Jordanhill Stone, Glasgow.

It is similar to the Nigg stone pattern, (page 21), but has an extra turn in the double straight-line spiral.

12　　　　**12**

R.A. 98

Some two bay arrangements with no or limited internal Z verticals.

A development of the simple edge pattern on the St Andrews Stone No.14.

Note the large internal S figures which develop in two bay or wider patterns.

All this develops from a fragment carved on the edge of a stone. Somehow the mason managed to minimise the thickness of the flags which the drawing portrays.

Finish.

Note that the side Z triangles have attachments but the top and bottom Z triangles do not.

Using the same setting-out, a two bay development of the St Vigean's one b[...]
pattern on page 11.

Stage 4 on page 15.

Again the Z tails are cut off top and bottom to facilitate the internal repeat.

Various middle and edge arrangements are possible, as is the case with many two bay or overall patterns.

Plate 1. Folio 17b from the *Lindisfarne Gospels*

Plate 2. Folio 95 from the *Lindisfarne Gospels*

In these one bay patterns the Z figures and border hooks both have attachments, producing quadruple straight-line spirals. R.A. 952

12

Like many key patterns carved on stone the end treatment is missing, and standard end treatment is added here. By doing so the completed pattern becomes a standard pattern.

Meigle No. 20, Tayside and others.

R.A. 951

In both patterns the 'swastika' centres are square.

Dupplin, near Forteviot, Tayside.

The St Andrews Stone, Fife. See page 22.

A two bay version of Meigle No.20 but with large-triangle Z figures.

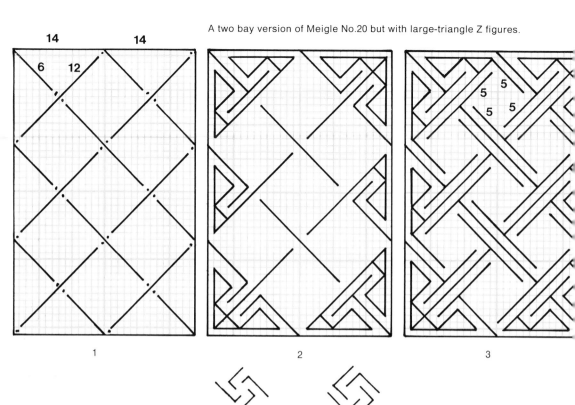

1

2

3

The 'swastika' centre is diamond if the diagonal size of the outer Z triangle is an odd number, and square if it is even.

4

5

6

Continue spirals inwardly to one unit.

A three bay version of the Meigle No.20 pattern, developing its full potential.

In the overall pattern you will see that one figure ⊐⊏ prevails.

Some previous one bay patterns in their small Z triangle (simplest) form.

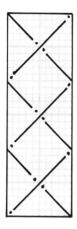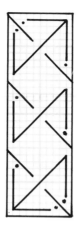

St Andrews No.14 (p.11)
Edge of Stone.

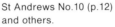

St Andrews No.10 (p.12)
and others.

St Vigeans No.12 (p.11)
Book of Kells folio 2V.

Norham. (p.13)

Burghead. (p.13)

At least two important stones use the small Z triangle. These are the Nigg stone and the St Andrews stone No.14 (back).

The Nigg stone, Easter Ross.

10 The top left hand corner is open, as shown here.

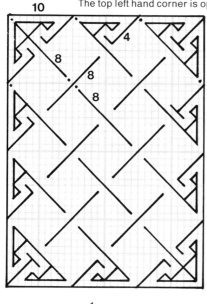

1

2

The interior consists entirely of ⌠ figures developing into double straight-line spirals 4.4.2.2

The Jordanhill pattern on page 14 is similar but with an extra turn in the spiral:- 5.5.3.3.1.1

3 and 4

Finish

The St Andrews stone No.14 is overleaf.

The St. Andrews stone No.14, Fife. (R.A. 963)

The actual pattern is 6 bays long.

It is a small triangle version of the Meigle pattern No.20 on page 17.

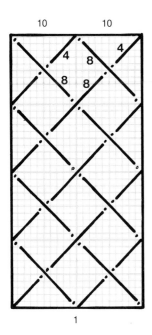

1

2

3

The top left corner is open as on the stone.

Figure 2 shows the standard corner treatment.

Figure 3 shows the special treatment used in the closed corners (Top right and bottom left.)

As on the Meigle stone No.20 on page 18, the interior consists entirely of quadruple straight-line spirals which are satisfying to draw.

4

5

6

A photograph of the stone is reproduced on page 17.

The Collieburn stone, Caithness. This requires large-triangle Z figures.

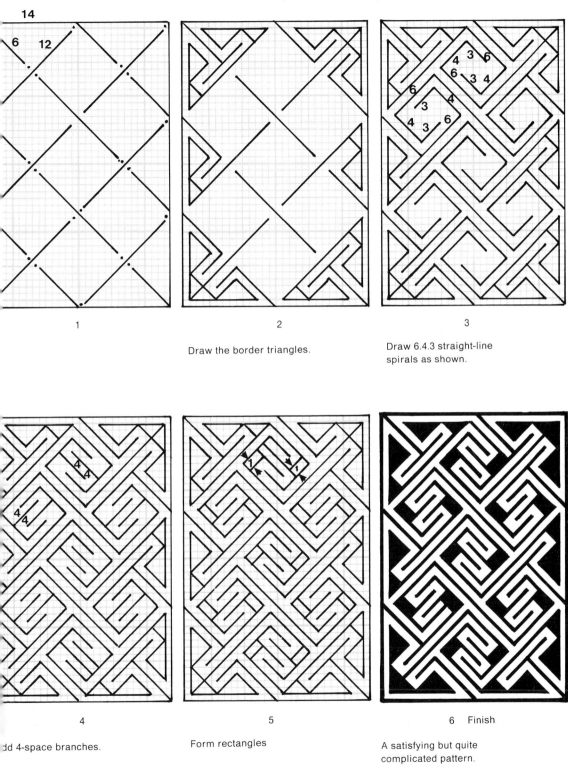

14

1

2

Draw the border triangles.

3

Draw 6.4.3 straight-line
spirals as shown.

4

dd 4-space branches.

5

Form rectangles

6   Finish

A satisfying but quite
complicated pattern.

Two complete patterns in the Book of Kells on folio IV. Right hand Column Head. (left hand opposite.) In this pattern the top left hand corner is closed.

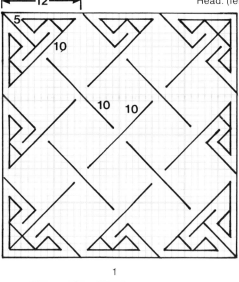

1

2

3

4

1 The main diagonals.
2 Start straight-line spirals.
3 Complete spirals as shown.
4 Draw internal triangles.

Finish.

Column head in the Book of Kells on folio IV. Left hand column. (R.H. on previous page.) In this pattern the top left hand corner is open.

1 The main diagonals.
2 Start the straight line spirals.
3 Complete the spirals as shown.

Finish.

Chapter 4

W Patterns

A mirrored development of the V pattern.

Romilly Allen attributes his pattern No.935 to Llantwit Major, Llangevelach, Glamorganshire and to Castle Dermot, Ireland.

12

Finish with straight line spirals without, or with, little triangles.

Romilly Allen attributes this pattern to Kells in Ireland. Overleaf it is developed into a two-triangle V pattern.

14

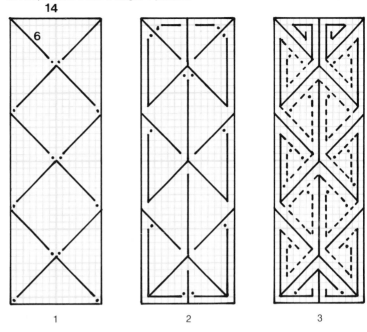

1   2   3

The straight-line spirals are best drawn together as illustrated above with dotted lines.

R.A. 936

Single triangle pattern,
Invergowrie, Angus.

4   5   6

The finished pattern without,
or with, small triangles.
Compare with the Invergowrie photograph alongside. They are not quite similar.

A single triangle pattern carved on a stone at Invergowrie, Angus.
See photograph on page 42.

A two triangle versio

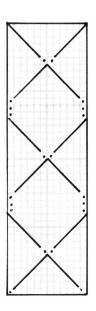
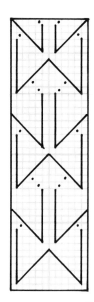
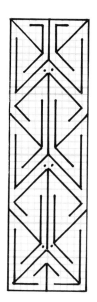

This three bay version using 2, 3 and 4 diagonal space triangles is in the Book
of Kells on folio 291 V and one bay versions are on the corners of folio 290 V.

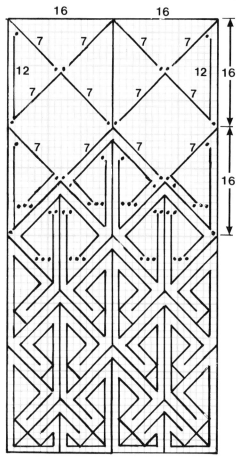

Shortage of space has necessitated a change of presentation.
The extra large △s are needed to break the internal vertical lines.

This three-triangle pattern is on folio 202 V in the Book of Kells with one small triangle as shown. See plate 6 facing page 49.

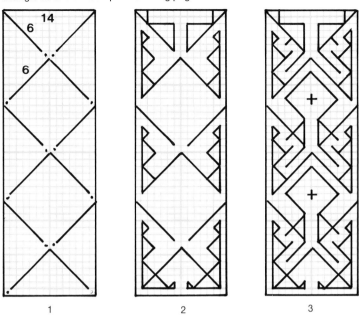

1   2   3

It can also be drawn with one large triangle without affecting the interior of the pattern, as shown on the two bay version overleaf.

4   5   Finish.

A two bay variation Book of Kells folio 202 V pattern but using three-diagonal triangles.

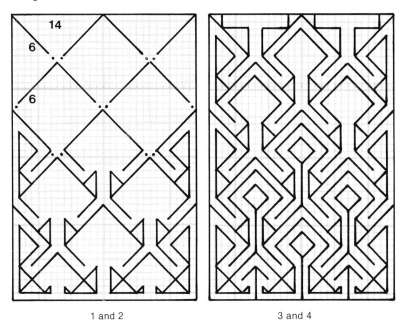

1 and 2   3 and 4

5   Finish.

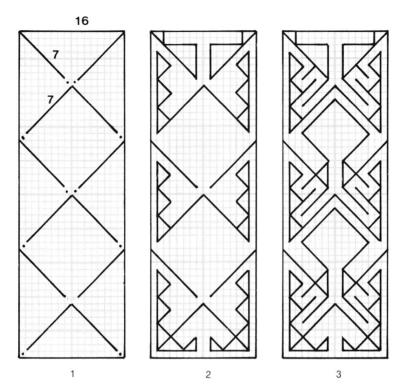

16

1   2   3

A further two-bay variation of the Book of Kells folio 202 V pattern, but using three two-diagonal triangles.

4   5   Finish.

This Z pattern is in the Book of Kells on folio 8 R. It is a mirrored and slightly stretched development of the one-bay key pattern on folio 4 R. (See page 12).

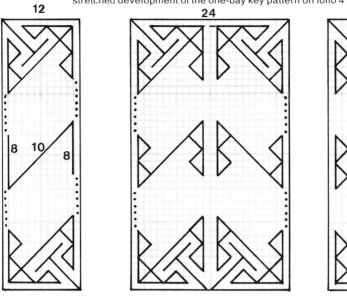

Draw 8.10.8 Zed figures with a vertical separation of six spaces.
The one bay figure is shown for guidance.

Plate 3. Folio 210b from the *Lindisfarne Gospels*

Plate 4. Folio 1v from the *Book of Kells*

Hook patterns

Like all key patterns, hook patterns can be rotated or mirrored.

Unlike Z patterns which consist mainly of double straight-line spirals, (there are some treble and quadruple straight-line spirals), hook patterns contain only single straight-line spirals.

This makes them easier to draw than Z patterns, but fewer different designs are possible.

In spite of their limited range, hook patterns have a charm of their own, particularly if they are over-painted in blocks of different colours as on folio 138 b in the Lindisfarne Gospels, included here on page 38. This particular illustration also explains my use of the title 'hook' for these patterns. The hooks are very pronounced.

3.2.2.1.1. Single straight-line spirals.

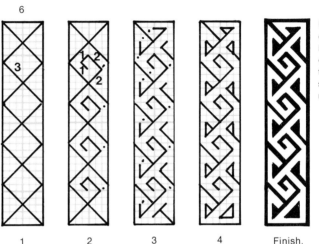

6

1   2   3   4   Finish.

Use spacer dots as before to ensure that full diagonal spacing is maintained.

As with knotwork, in the interest of constant white-path thickness, the finished line treatment should be outside the border lines and straddle the diagonal path lines.

3.3.2.2.1.1. A two unit development.

The stone carvers favoured straight-line spiral borders. The Lindisfarne scribe used dark triangles.

12

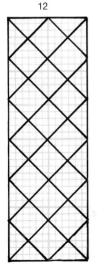

Romilly Allen likened hook patterns to the boughs of a tre branching out from a zig-zag stem.

These branches fill a three unit wide pattern which can be three or more units long.

Repeating branches aid the construction of overall patterns.

See also the block-coloured reproduction facing page 32 of the key patterns on folio 210 b of the Lindisfarne Gospels.

A wider version.

The previous pattern turned on its side so that the 'branches' are hanging.

A non-standard pattern is reconstructed on page 61 using diagonal setting-out. The subject is the key pattern on the Rosemarkie stone No.1, Ross-shire.

A 3 space shift in the pattern position, vertically and horizontally, showing different border treatment.

This is standard rendering of the three unit wide pattern featured in the Lindisfarne Gospels on folio 138 b. See also the four unit wide patterns on folio 210 b, plate 3 facing page 32.

3.2.2.1.1

Pictish Edging

Triangular edging
as used in the manuscr

Another version of the same pattern

4.4.3.3.2.2.1.1.

The Farr stone, Caithness
(and others).

The same with
triangular edging.

Note that in the 4 (even number) grid unit the spiral starts in the centre of the
setting-out square.

The Lindisfarne Gospels, folio 95.
The bottom key pattern.

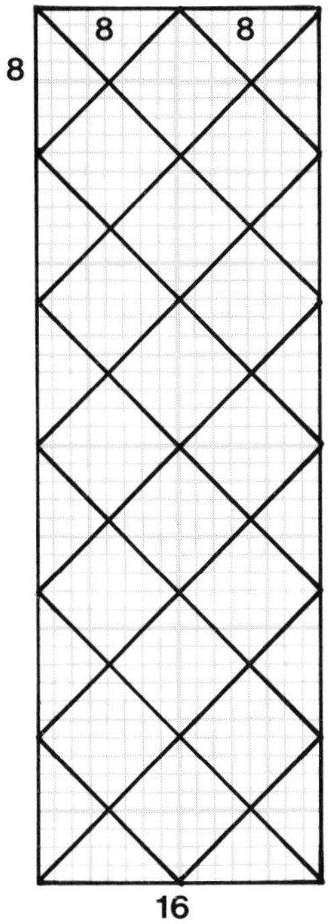

4.3.3.2.2.1.1

8

8   8

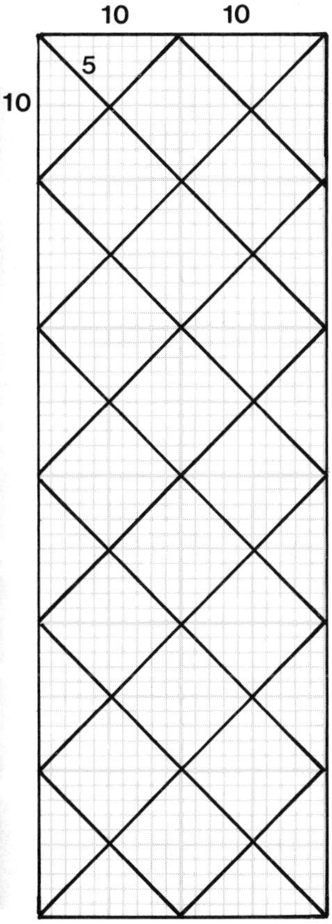

Six units long.

The original is eleven units long.

16

The side key pattern.

10   10

10

5

Pictish border treatment.

5.4.4.3.3.2.2.1.1

Six units long.
The original is thirteen units long.

20

37

5mm graph paper is also suitable for drawing Celtic hook patterns, as demonstrated below by a quarter of the pattern on folio 138b of the Lindisfarne Gospels.

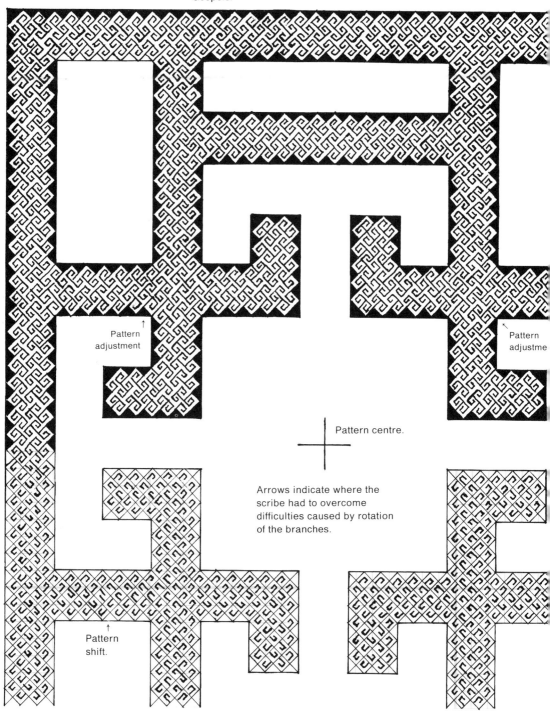

Pattern adjustment

Pattern adjustme

Pattern centre.

Arrows indicate where the scribe had to overcome difficulties caused by rotation of the branches.

Pattern shift.

The lower portion illustrates the hooks attached to the diagonal lines.

Nowhere is the pattern wider than three units.

Doubling the scale on 5mm graph paper, using the hanging branch pattern on page 35.

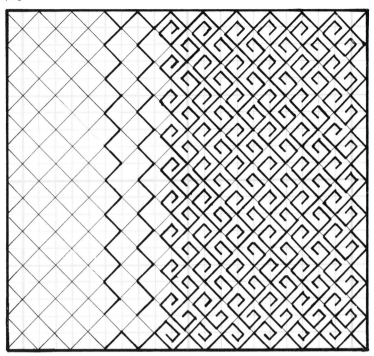

Try this different arrangement.

The upper key-type pattern on folio 94 b in the Lindisfarne Gospels.

The standard version, 6 units long. The superfluous border △s are omitted her

The setting-out squares are 6 diagonal spaces long.

The original design is 10 units long.

The flag sides are 3 units long.

The original confirms the narrow horizontal spacing arrowed.

In the actual version the flag sides are 4 units long as below.

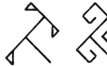

The lower pattern is basically the same but has only one 'horizontal' row of triangles.

This type of pattern is a variation of the hook pattern as illustrated alongside.

Chapter 6
Small patterns

Some small motif patterns from MSS and stone carvings. The locations are many, particularly in Wales.

A very simple pattern, made possible by the small triangles in the corners.

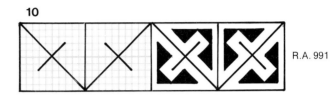

R.A. 986

These small patterns were often linked together.

10

R.A. 991

R.A. 992

10

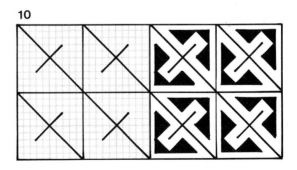

Unneeded vertical and horizontal lines may be erased.

Finish

A small △ version

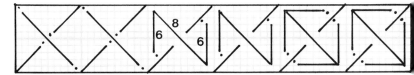

This is a similar pattern but the T head is broader.

St. Andrews, Fife and Invergowrie, Tayside.

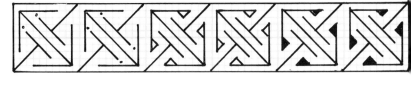

An overall version with internal verticals and horizontals.

The internal vertical and horizontal lines may be omitted.

Small triangle, Invergowrie, Angus. No.1 and St. Andrews, Fife, No.7.

These patterns are not listed by Romilly Allen.

The Z figure. 2 triangle.

R.A. 987

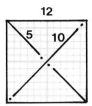

The pattern repeated.

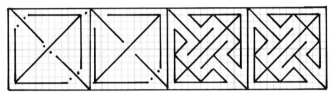

Overall versions.

Internal vertical and horizontal lines may be added.

Pattern repeats must be in pairs so that opposite corners of the overall pattern are similar.

4 triangle Z figure   R.A. 989

20

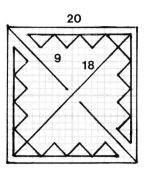

9   18

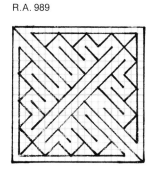

Try also 3 triangle version R.A. 988 opposite.

24

5 triangle Z figures.

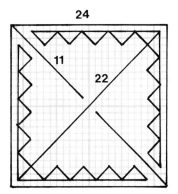

11

22

The 5 triangle figures give alternative arrangements.

Finish   R.A. 990   Finish

More Z motifs.

All can be repeated in both directions, see previous pages.

10

14

Nevern, Pembrokeshire

R.A. 988

16

Book of Kells
folio 5 R.

Some motifs with X centres.

R.A. 995

Fairly common
including
Llanwit Major
Glamorganshire
and St Andrews
Fife.

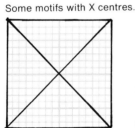

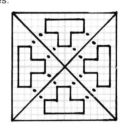

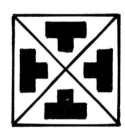

R.A. 996

R.A. 997

Two variations.

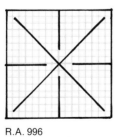

Left, Lindisfarne and
Almouth,
Northumberland.

Right, the Gospels
of MacDurnan.

Some diamond shaped motifs.
The Book of Kells folio 3 R

Finish with or without the ring.

The Book of Kells folio 277 V

A ring can be added if desired.

The normal 2 triangle version.

These patterns are attributed by Romilly mostly to Wales.

14

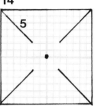

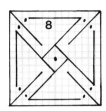

R.A. 1010

Draw 5 space diagonals.

Form the eccentric Z figures.

Add the triangles and tails.

Finish.
Golden Grove,
Carmarthen.

18

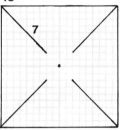

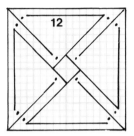

R.A. 1011

Draw 7 space diagonals.

Form the eccentric Z figures

Complete with three triangles

Finish.
Margam, Glamorgan.

A two triangle version without the central square. This was attributed by Romilly Allen to Barrochan and St Andrews in Scotland, Clonmacnois in Ireland, and Margam and Nevern in Wales.

14

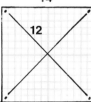

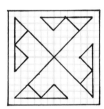

R.A. 1009
Finish

This pattern was attributed by Romilly Allen to the Gospels of MacDurnan.

22

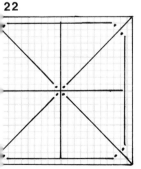

R.A. 1003

Chapter 7

Panel shapes, treatments and embellishments.

A simple corner.

A border version.

Compare with the $\frac{1}{2}$ Z (V) pattern on page 2.

Plate 5. Folio 2v from the *Book of Kells*

Plate 6. Folio 202v from the *Book of Kells*

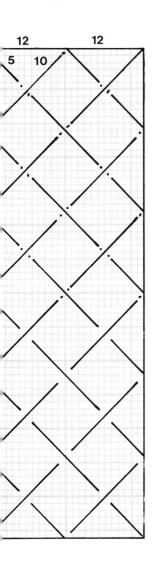

12   **12**

5   **10**

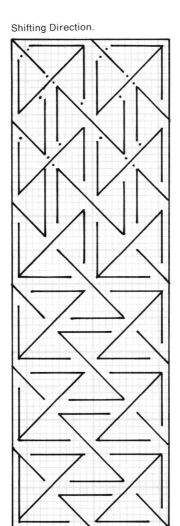

A good example is in The Book of Kells on folio 8 R.

There is a subtle difference
between the two patterns.
On the right each square
is repeated.

One of the corner patterns on
folio 210 b in the Lindisfarne
Gospels. It is reproduced on
Plate 3 facing page 32.

This is a good example of the
use of blocks of different
background colours on key
patterns.

White path centre-lines.

Wide border paths are drawn to accommodate these.

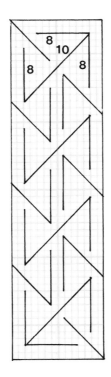

The finished design, working inside the border setting-out lines to aid the uniformity of path widths.

This doubled key pattern Z figure is a variation of the topmost pattern on page 47. Jedburgh, Roxburghshire.

Chapter 8
Diagonal setting-out.

We now abandon graph paper and proceed with plain paper.

As with knotwork, the ancient scribes and stone carvers would have been unlikely to create a pattern within a chosen panel space. It is more likely that they would select or create a suitable pattern in its standard form and adjust this to suit the panel space.

Since most of the lines in key patterns are diagonal any departure of these from 45° affects the vertical and horizontal line spacing, making graph paper unsuitable for setting-out and diagonal setting-out essential.

The Picts were familiar with the 3.4.5 right angled which is used in the following example.

The one bay Z pattern.

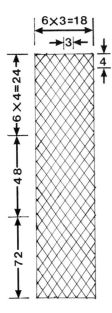

An internal arrangement, using the Burghead pattern illustrated on page 13.

An irregular shape.

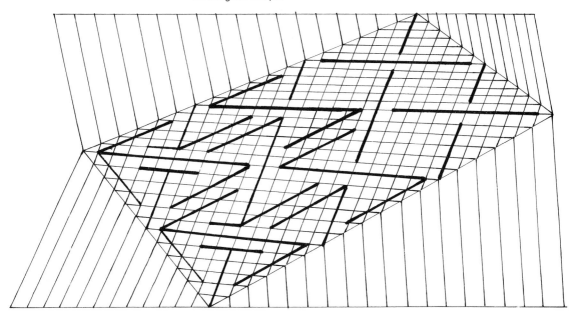

The 12 × 18 two-bay panel can be subdivided by ruler and set square as shown. The measured construction lines need not be horizontal as shown here for tidiness.

Alternatively a pocket calculator can be used. For preference the side spacing should be longer than the end spacing.

The finished pattern can be imagined as paving viewed in perspective.

An annular Z pattern.

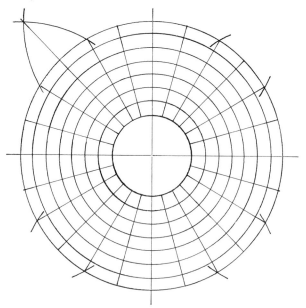

Draw a circle with a radius of 10 units. Using the radius divide the circle into 1⁶
and then 24 segments.

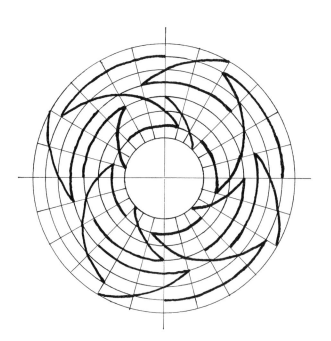

Draw 4.5.4 Z figures and 4.3 half Z figures as shown.

Add the Z triangles.

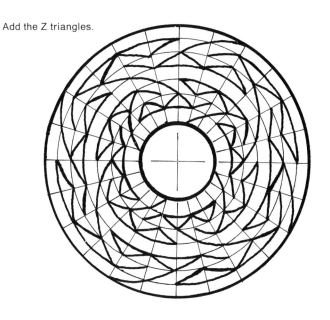

It is important to slightly curve the triangle sides in keeping with the curved Z figures.

The finished pattern.

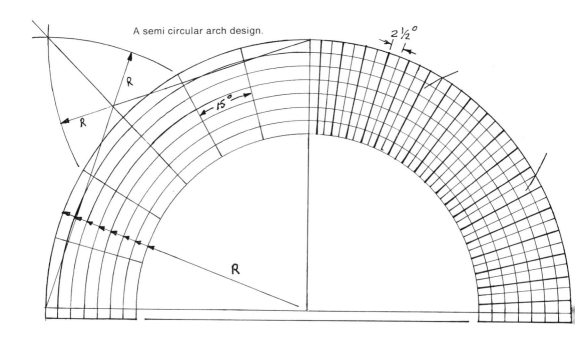

A semi circular arch design.

Draw the arch outer radius R, in this case 80 units, and draw inner half-circles 4 units apart. Sub-divide the arch into 6 and then 72 segments, by compass as shown, or by protractor.

Add an extra half segment to the base at each side. This is needed to balance the pattern and obtain a level base. It would not be necessary if the border paths were half the thickness of the middle paths, as usually drawn on rectangular patterns.

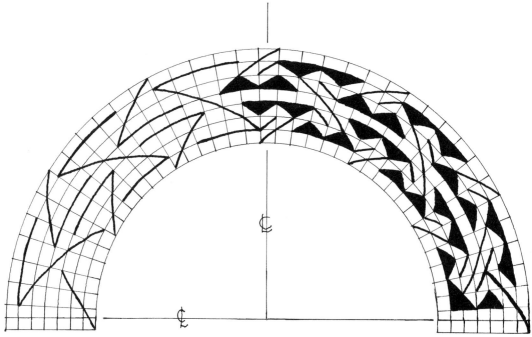

The Z figures and the finished pattern. The triangle sides should be slightly curved.

An arched hook pattern.

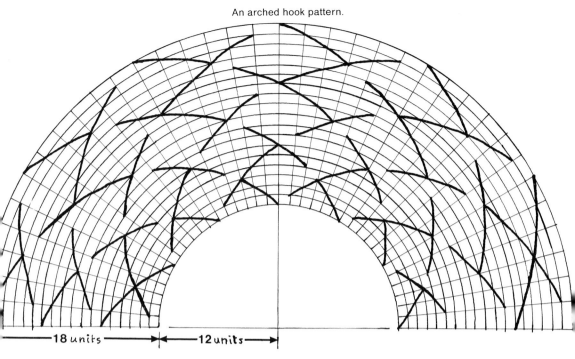

——18 units——⟩⟨——12 units——⟩

The semi-circle is divided into six and then thirty-six segments. The chosen radius is thirty units but may be varied.

This is a curved version of the hook pattern on page 36.

An oval pattern.

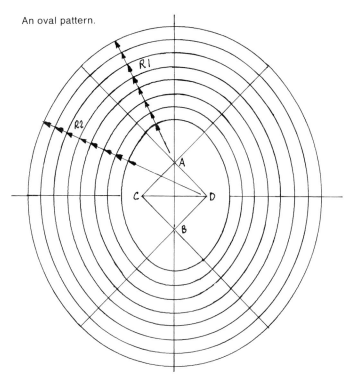

Draw vertical and horizontal centre lines and mark points A, B, C and D, in this case 20 units apart on the centre lines.

From points A and B draw 45° diagonal lines as shown.

From points A, B, C and D draw rings as shown, in this case 4 units apart radially.

Below, sub-divide each sector by 3, making 24 sectors.

The sectors must be divisible by 6 to draw a continuous Z pattern.

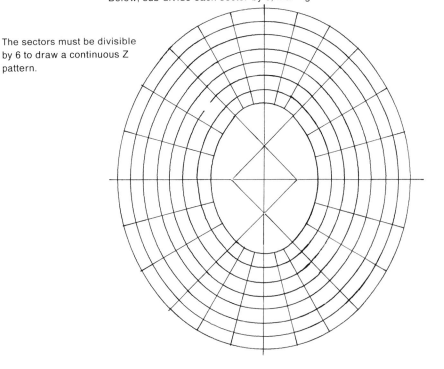

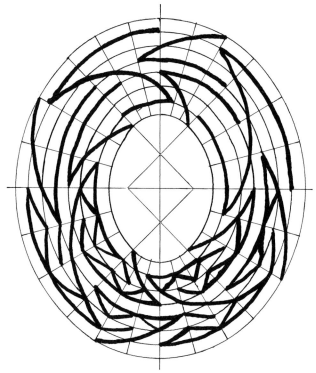

Draw the Z and half Z figures, followed by the triangles.

The finished design. The varying curved Z figures bring a new dimension to key patterns. It is important to slightly curve the triangle sides in keeping with the curved Z figures. In this case the construction lines have been retained.

The central setting-out figure need not be square. The pattern space is seven units wide.

The finished pattern. Again it is important to slightly curve the triangle sides in keeping with the curved Z figures. In this case the construction lines have been retained.

An attempted construction of the key pattern on the Rosemarkie stone No.1, Easter Ross.

It is based on Romilly Allen's version which is illustrated on page 0.

The slope of the original pattern is less than shown here.

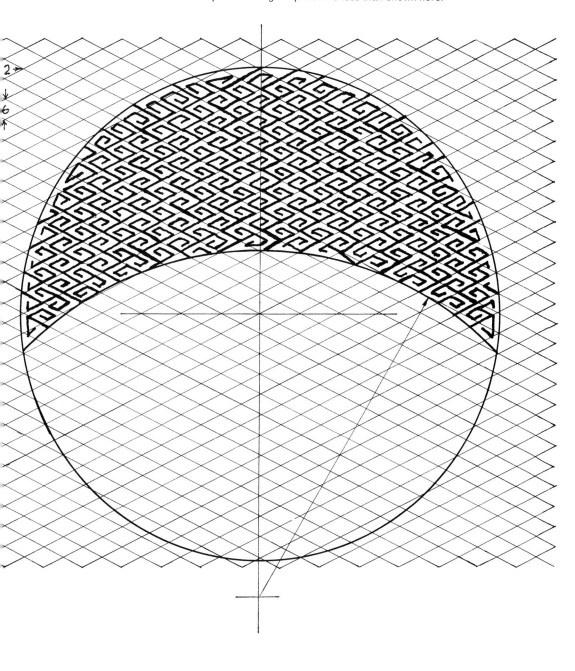

Appendix: extract from *Early Christian Monuments* by J. Romilly Allen

ANALYSIS OF KEY-PATTERNS, WITH THE LOCALITIES—*continued.*

No. 923.—An irregular surface key-pattern of the same class as the preceding.

Rothesay, No. 1.

The geographical distribution of the square patterns, more especially those of the Greek fret type, show that they are more common in Mercian England and North Wales than in Scotland or Ireland. This points to their being Saxon or Carlovingian imitations of classical originals. The Scotic designers always show a preference for the diagonal key-patterns.

Diagonal Key-Patterns filling Rectangular Spaces (Nos. 924 to 1012).

No. 924.—Key-pattern formed of ⋁ shaped bars placed thus ⋁ ⋀ ⋁ ⋀, and having the triangles filled in with single straight-line spirals.

Isle of Man—
    Kirk Maughold.

Meigle, No. 6.

No. 925.—Key-pattern formed of ⟋⟍ shaped bars placed thus ⟋⟍ ⟋⟍ ⟋⟍, and having the triangles filled in with single straight-line spirals.

Meigle, No. 24.

No. 926.—The same as No. 925, but with the ⟋⟍ shaped bars placed thus ⟍⟋⟍, and having the triangles filled in with double straight-line spirals.

Rosemarkie, No. 2.	St Andrews, No. 21.	*Wales*—
Drainie, No. 10.		Llandrinio, Montgomeryshire.
St Vigean's, No. 4.		Llandevaelog, Brecknockshire.
Meigle, No. 29.	*England*—	
St Andrews, No. 7.	St Erth, Cornwall.	*MSS.*—
„ No. 9.	Sancreed, „	Psalter of St Augustine.

No. 927.—The same as No. 925, but with the angles of the straight-line spirals filled in with small black triangles (No. 865).

Metalwork—Domnach Airgid.

No. 928.—The same as No. 926, but finished off with two small black triangles to each bay (No. 867).

MSS.—Lichfield, St Chad's Gospels.

No. 929.—The same as No. 926, but finished off with three small black triangles to each bay (No. 868).

Ireland—
Clonmacnois.

MSS.—
British Museum, Harl. 2788.
„ „ Bede's Eccl. Hist. (Tib., C. ii.).
„ „ Psalter (Vesp., A. i.).

No. 930.—The same as No. 926, but finished off with five small black triangles to each bay (No. 870)

MSS.—British Museum, Bibl. Reg., I. E. vi.

No. 931.—The same as No. 926, but finished off with five small black triangles to each bay in a similar way to No. 869.

MSS.—St Gall.

Plate 7. Folio 290v from the *Book of Kells*

Plate 8. Folio 291v from the *Book of Kells*

No. 932.—Produced by doubling No. 928, thus giving a series of ⟋⟍ and ⟍ shaped bars arranged thus

⟋⟍ ⇌ ⟋⟍, and finished off with two small black triangles to each bay (No. 867).

Kirriemuir, No. 1.	*MSS.*—	*Metalwork*—
Invergowrie, No. 1.	St Gall Gospels.	Mus. R.I.A.—Plaque with
Rosemarkie, No. .	St Chad's Gospels.	crucifixion.
	Book of Kells.	

No. 933.—The same as No. 932, but finished off with three small black triangles to each bay (No. 869).

Inchcolm.	*Ivories*—
Gattonside.	St Genoel's Elderen, Limburg (Diptych).
Ireland—	
Clonmacnois.	
MSS.—	*Metalwork*—
British Museum, Psalter (Vit., F. xi.).	Bronze Bell found at Cashel, now at
Dimma's Book.	Adare Manor.

No. 934.—The same as No. 932, but with large black squares in the centre instead of pairs of smaller ones.

MSS.—St Gall Gospels.

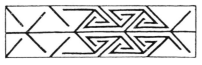

No. 935.—Key-pattern composed of —⟨ and ⟋ shaped bars arranged thus —⟨ ⇌ —⟨ and
the triangles filled in with double straight-line spirals (No. 862A).

Wales—	*Ireland*—
Llantwit Major, Glamorganshire.	Castle Dermot.
Llangevelach, ,,	

No. 936.—Key-pattern, produced by doubling No. 926, composed of —< and ∧ shaped bars arranged thus —< ∨ —<, and the triangles filled in with double straight-line spirals (No. 862A).

Ireland—Kells.

No. 937.—The same as No. 935, but with the central vertical bar not continuous, and each bay finished off with two small black triangles (No. 867).

MSS.—Book of Kells.

No. 938.—The same as No. 937, but with each of the outside bays finished off with three small black triangles, and the central bays finished off with small black squares and single black triangles.

MSS.—Book of Kells.

No. 939.—The same as No. 936, but with large black squares introduced in every other bay in the centre.

MSS.—St John's Coll., Cambridge, Irish Psalter.

No. 940.—Key-pattern composed of Z and ∧ shaped bars arranged thus Z∧∨Z, and finished off with pairs of small black triangles (No. 867) and large squares in the centre.

Govan.

England—
Lanivet, Cornwall.

Wales—
Penally, Pembrokeshire.

MSS.—
St John's Coll., Cambridge (Irish Psalter).

No. 941.—Key-pattern composed of Z and ∧ shaped bars arranged thus Z ∧∨ Z, and each outer bay finished off with pairs of small black triangles (No. 867) and each central bay with pairs of black rectangles.

Kildalton (quadrant of ring of cross).

England—
Hurworth, now at Durham.
Norham, Northumberland.

Ireland—
Kells.

No. 942.—The same as No. 941, but with each of the outer bays finished off with three small black triangles (No. 868) and the central bays with bars branching at right angles, like the teeth of a rack.

Crieff.

No. 943.—The same as No. 941, but the central bays each finished off with two large black triangles (No. 843).

Burghead, No. 10A.

No. 944.—Key-pattern formed of ◁ and ∧ shaped bars arranged thus ◁∨ ∨∧ ◁∨, and finished off as in No. 943.

St Vigean's, No. 12.

No. 945.—The same as No. 944, but with the pairs of black triangles which finish off the central bays placed with the white space between them vertically instead of horizontally.

St Andrews, No. 10.   Govan, No. 34.

No. 946.—The same as No. 945, but with the central bays each finished off with a pair of black rectangles instead of triangles.

St Andrews, No. 14.

No. 947.—The same as No. 945, but with the central bays finished off with double spirals.

MSS.—Lambeth Lib.—Gospels of MacDurnan.

No. 948.—The same as No. 947, but with the outer bays finished off with sets of four small black triangles (No. 869).

MSS.—
Book of Armagh.
Gospels of MacDurnan.

No. 949. — Key-pattern formed of ⟋ ⟍ and ⟍ shaped bars arranged thus ⟋⟍ ⟍⟋ ⟋⟍, and having every other square bay in the centre filled in with double spirals and the remaining triangles with double straight-line spirals.

Ireland—
Monasterboice.

No. 950. — Key-pattern formed of ⟋ and ⟍ shaped bars arranged thus ⟋⟍ ⟍⟋ ⟋⟍, and having the square bays in the centre filled with triple spirals and the remaining triangles with double straight-line spirals finished off with pairs of small black triangles (No. 867).

Dupplin.

Isle of Man—
Kirk Bride.

No. 951.—The same as No. 950, ~~but~~ with the square bays in the centre filled in with quadruple straight-line spirals having forked-branch terminations.

Dupplin.

No. 952.—The same as No. 951, but without the forked-branch terminations to the quadruple straight-line spirals.

Farnell.
Dunblane.
Meigle, No. 20.
England—
 Lanivet, Cornwall.
Wales—
 Penally, Pembrokeshire.

No. 953.—The same as No. 952, but with the ends of the quadruple straight-line spirals in the square central bays meeting in a point, and the remaining triangular bays finished off with pairs of small black triangles (No. 867).

MSS.—British Museum, Harl. 2788.

No. 954.[1]—The same as No. 941, but with the square central bays completely filled in with black, and the triangular bays finished off with sets of four small black triangles (No. 869).

MSS.—Lambeth Lib.—Gospels of MacDurnan.

No. 955.—Key-pattern formed of ⋋ and ⋀ shaped bars arranged thus ⋋⋁⋌, and having the square central bays filled in with double straight-line spirals and the triangular bays finished off with pairs of small black triangles (No. 867).

Ireland.—Kells.

---

[1] This pattern is out of its right order and should have come immediately after No. 943.

No. 956.—Key-pattern composed of ╲╱ and ╱╲ shaped bars arranged thus , and having the square central bays filled in with double straight-line spirals and the triangular bays with single straight-line spirals.

Kilmartin.

No. 957.—Key-pattern composed of ⟨ and ╲╱ shaped bars arranged thus , and having the square and triangular bays both filled in with single straight-line spirals.

Kingoldrum.

We have now arrived at the point when the patterns cease to be mere borders and become surface-patterns adapted to fill large rectangular panels. Nos. 958 to 984 are all surface key-patterns. It seems probable that the surface-patterns were developed out of the borders by doubling, trebling, or quadrupling them, otherwise the complicated arrangements of the bars, forming the basis of the pattern so as to make them interlock correctly at regular intervals whilst meandering over the entire area, would not have been easily hit upon. It will be seen that, in consequence of the setting-out lines of the pattern being placed diagonally with regard to the margin, the angles of the ⟨ or ⟨ shaped bars have to be altered to suit it, thus converting them into 7 and ⟨. The latter no doubt suggested the ⟨⟩ shaped bar which forms the basis of the most characteristic of all the Celtic key-patterns, viz., No. 974.

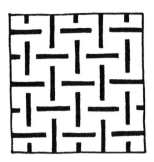

No. 829 repeated.

No. 829A repeated.

No. 958.—Surface key-pattern based on ⟨ shaped bars interlocked as in No. 829A, and of same type as border-pattern No. 941, but with plain double straight-line spirals filling the squares.

Ulbster.	Burghead, No. 12.	Kilmartin.
Nigg.	Aberlemno, No. 3.	
Canna.	Ardchattan.	*England*—
Burghead, No. 9.	Abercorn.	Norham, Northumberland.

No. 959.—Surface key-pattern based on the same arrangement of bars as No. 958, but with the square bays filled in as in border key-pattern No. 942 and finished off with two small black rectangles.

Collieburn.

No. 960.—Surface key-pattern based on the same arrangement of bars as No. 958, and corresponding with border key-pattern No. 941, except that the square bays are finished off with black triangles instead of black rectangles.

Rosemarkie, No. 1.

No. 961.—The same as No. 960, but adapted for a panel two bays instead of one and a half bays in width.

No. 962.—A combination of No. 961 with No. 936.

MSS.—Book of Kells.

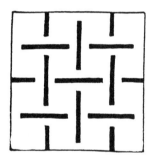

No. 832 repeated.

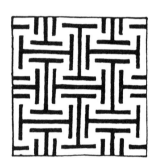

No. 832A repeated

No. 963.—Surface key-pattern based on ⟋ shaped bars interlocked as in No. 832A and

of same type as border key-pattern No. 952.

| St Andrews, No. 14. Mugdrum. Rosemarkie, No. 1. | *Wales—* Penally, Pembrokeshire. | *MSS.—* British Museum, Harl. 2788. St Gall Gospels. |

No. 964.—This is really more of a diaper than a key-pattern, and it is only placed here because the panel is the same size as in No. 963. The surface is divided into squares by diagonal lines. Each square is filled with a cruciform figure made by placing four small black squares at the angles of a central square. The triangular bays round the edge are filled in with a figure made up of three small black triangles.

Nigg.
MSS.—Book of Kells.

No. 965.—Surface key-pattern of same type as border key-pattern No. 957, based on bars branching out like the boughs of a tree from a zigzag stem (No. 837A).

Meigle, No. 6.

No. 837 repeated.

No. 837A repeated.

No. 966.—The same class of pattern as No. 965, but two bays in width instead of one and a half, and having the triangular bays round the edge filled in with black.

MSS.—
   Bodleian Lib., Oxford—Gospels of Mac-Regol.

No. 967.—The same class of pattern as No. 965, but of the same width as No. 966.

Kirriemuir.
Monifieth, No. 1.
Strathmartine, No. 3.
St Vigean's, No. 2.
Dunkeld, No. 3.

Meigle, No. 7.
  ,,   No. 24.
  ,,   No. 28.
Ireland—
Kells.

No. 968.—The same class of pattern as No. 966, but three bays wide instead of two.

MSS.—
    Gospels of MacRegol.
    Lindisfarne Gospels.

No. 969.—The same class of pattern as No. 967, but three bays wide instead of two.

    Farr.
    Rosemarkie, No. 1.
    Kettins.
    Strathmartine, No. 2.
    St Andrews, No. 4.
    Inchbrayock.

No. 970.—The same class of pattern as No. 968, but four bays in width instead of three.

MSS.—
    Lindisfarne Gospels.

No. 970A (no diagram).—The same class of pattern as No. 969, but four bays in width instead of three.

    Golspie.
    Nigg.

No. 971.—Pattern of the same class as No. 969, on the arm of cross.

    Lothbeg.
    Reay.
    Aberlemno, No. 2.
    St Vigean's, No. 7.
    Fowlis Wester.
    Meigle, No. 3.
      ,,   No. 5.
    St Madoes, No. 1.

No. 828c repeated.

No. 972.—Pattern of the same class as No. 968, except that the branches from each adjacent pair of trees interlock and form double spirals instead of single ones (compare with No. 828c). The ends of the branches are finished off with black triangles.

MSS.—Lindisfarne Gospels.

No. 972A (no diagram).—The same as No. 972, but with bosses and spiral-work in the square bays.

Iona, No. 2.
,, No. 3.
,, No. 5.

No. 972B.—Diagram showing various methods of interlocking surface key-patterns.

No. 973.[1]—The same as No. 958, but three bays wide instead of two, and with the ends of the straight-line spirals in the square bays joined together.

Wales—
Silian, Cardiganshire.

No. 974.   No. 975.

Nos. 974 to 976.—Surface key-patterns based on ⟍Z⟋ shaped bars corresponding to border key-pattern No. 932.

Farr [2] (4 bays by 4 bays).
Reay (8 bays by 8 bays).
Rosemarkie, No. 1 (9 bays by 9 bays).
     ,,   No. 2 (5 bays by 3 bays).
Shandwick (5 bays).
St Vigean's, No. 24.
Meigle, No. 4.
St Andrews, No. 1.
     ,,   No. 7.
     ,,   No. 8.
     ,,   No. 14.

St Andrews, No. 20.

MSS.—
St Chad's Gospels.
Book of Kells.
Lindisfarne Gospels.
Gospels of MacDurnan.

Metalwork—
Bronze Buckle found at Islandbridge near Dublin.

[1] This pattern is out of its proper order and should have followed No. 958.

[2] The number of bays in the width of the panel and the ways of finishing off the pattern with little black triangles varies in the different examples specified.

No. 976.—In this case the ⟍⟋ bars do not all run in the same direction.

MSS.—
  Book of Kells.
  Lindisfarne Gospels.

No. 977.—Surface key-pattern corresponding to border-pattern No. 952, but with two of the bars of the quadruple straight-line spirals joined together.

Ireland—
  Kells.

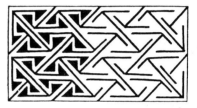

No. 978.—The same type of pattern as No. 974, but with triangular bays finished off with pairs of black triangles.

MSS.—
  Gospels of MacRegol.

No. 979.—Surface key-pattern of same type as border key-pattern No. 935.

Wales—
  Llantwit Major, Glamorganshire.

No. 980.—Surface key-pattern of same type as border key-pattern No. 937.

  Nigg.
  Tullibole.

No. 981.—Surface key-pattern of same type as border key-pattern No. 940.

MSS.—
   St Gall Gospels.

No. 982.—Surface key-pattern of same type as border key-pattern No. 947, but with double straight-line spirals in the square bays.

Drainie, No. 15.
England—
   Irton, Cumberland.

No. 983.—Surface key-pattern of same type as border key-pattern No. 956.

No. 984.—The same type of pattern as No. 958, but with the central row of square bays divided into two triangles and filled in with single straight-line spirals, and having the triangular bays round the outside finished off with sets of three small black triangles (No. 868).

Jordanhill.   Nigg.

The remaining key-patterns adapted to fill rectangular spaces may be called diaper key-patterns, since the setting out lines both horizontally and

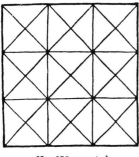

No. 873 repeated.

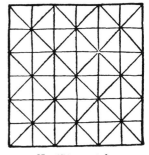

No. 874 repeated.

vertically and also in the direction of the two diagonals of a square (Nos. 873 and 874), thus produce the star-like appearance where the lines meet in a point, as in the diaper surface ornament of Gothic architecture.

Nos. 985 to 990, 995 to 999, 1002 and 1003, and Nos. 1007 to 1012 occur usually in isolated squares, but they can also be repeated to form a border or surface-pattern.

No. 985.—A square divided diagonally into two triangles and filled in with double straight-line spirals.

Wales—Margam, Glamorganshire.

No. 986.—A square divided diagonally into two triangles and filled in with a figure formed of three small black triangles, there being a short bar crossing the diagonal bar in the centre at right angles.

No. 987.—A square divided diagonally into two triangles and filled in with ⌐ and ⌐ shaped bars placed thus ⌐, each bay being finished off with pairs of black triangles (No. 867).

Drainie, No. 11.
St Vigean's, No. 15.
England—
    Lindisfarne, Northumberland.
MSS.—
    St Chad's Gospels.
    Book of Kells.
    British Museum, Psalter (Vit., F. xi.).

No. 988.—The same as No. 987, but having each bay finished off with sets of three small black triangles (No. 868).

Wales—
    Nevern, Pembrokeshire.

MSS.—
    Gospels of MacDurnan.

No. 989.—The same as No. 987, but having each bay finished off with sets of four small black triangles.

MSS.—Gospels of MacDurnan.

No. 990.—The same as No. 987, but having each bay finished off with sets of five small black triangles.

MSS.—St Gall Gospels.

No. 991.—Border key-pattern formed by repeating No. 986 in a single vertical row, the diagonals of the squares facing alternately to the right and to the left.

Wales—
　　Llantwit Major, Glamorganshire.
　　Carew, Pembrokeshire.
　　Golden Grove, Carmarthenshire.

No. 992.—Formed by doubling No. 991.

Wales—
　　Nevern, Pembrokeshire.
　　Golden Grove, Carmarthenshire.

No. 993.—Formed by repeating No. 988 in a single vertical row.

Ireland—	*MSS.—*
Monasterboice.	British Museum, Harl. 2788.

No. 994.—Formed by doubling No. 993.

Dogtown.	Keills.

No. 994A (no diagram).—The same as No. 994, but with three vertical rows instead of two.

England—	*MSS.—*
Irton, Cumberland.	Gospels of MacDurnan.

No. 995.—A square divided into eight triangles, each filled in with single straight-
line spirals.

Berneray.
Invergowrie, No. 1.
St Andrews, No. 7.
　　,,　　No. 9.
Wales—
Llantwit Major, Glamorganshire.
Llangevelach,　　　,,
Ireland—
Termonfechin.
Tuam.

No. 996.—The same as No. 995, but with
four of the bars lapping over so as to form
a swastica in the centre.

England—
Lindisfarne, Northumberland.
Alnmouth,　　　　,,

No. 997.—The same as No.
995, but with each triangular
bay finished off with pairs of
small black triangles.

MSS.—
Gospels of MacDurnan.

No. 998.—The same as No.
995, but with each triangular
bay finished off with sets of
three small black triangles.

MSS.—
St Gall Penitentiale.

No. 999.—A variation of No.
995, produced by doubling
some of the lines.

Wales—
Maen Achwyfan, Flintshire.

No. 1000.—Formed by the repetition of No.
995 in a single vertical row.

England—
Stainton-le-Street, now at Durham.

No. 1001.—Formed by repeating No. 995 in a double
vertical row, with some variations in the centre.

Wales—Penmon, Anglesey.
Ireland—St Brecan's Bed, Aran Mór.

No. 1002.—Square divided into eight triangles, each filled in with double straight-line spirals. It differs from No. 995 in having the two bars which cross in the centre placed thus ✚ instead of ✕. The lower right-hand quarter of the square in No. 1002 corresponds with the upper left-hand quarter of the square in No. 995.

No. 1003.—The same as No. 1002, but with each bay finished off with pairs of small black triangles.

MSS.—Gospels of MacDurnan.

No. 1004.—Pattern formed by repeating No. 1002 in a single vertical row.

Monifieth, No. 1.
Dupplin.
England—
Lindisfarne, Northumberland.

No. 1005.—A combination of No. 1004 and No. 994.

Ireland—
Monasterboice.

No. 1006.—Formed by repeating No. 981 in two vertical rows as in No. 994, but with the figures in each bay facing alternately in opposite directions.

Monifieth.

No. 1007.—A square divided into four triangles and each filled in with single straight-line spirals all having the same direction of twist.

Wales—
Merthyr Mawr, Glamorganshire.
Margam, Glamorganshire.

No. 1008.—A square divided into four triangles and each filled in with No. 868 arranged swastica fashion.

England—
Stonegrave, Yorkshire.

No. 1009.—A square divided into four triangles and each filled in with No. 867 arranged swastica fashion.

Barrochan.
St Andrews.
Ireland—Clonmacnois.
Wales—
Margam, Glamorganshire.
Nevern, Pembrokeshire.

No. 1010.—The same as No. 1009, but with a black square in the centre.

Wales—Golden Grove, Carmarthenshire.

No. 1011.—The same as No. 1010, but with each bay finished off with three small black triangles (No. 868) instead of two (No. 867).

Wales—
Margam, Glamorganshire.

No. 1012.—A square divided into four triangles and each filled in with No. 867 arranged swastica fashion.

Wales—
Nevern, Pembrokeshire.

Key-Patterns adapted for filling Circular and Annular Spaces (*Nos. 1013 to 1022A*).

No. 1013.—Key-pattern of same type as No. 969, with single straight-line spirals branching from a zigzag stem like a tree.

Eassie.	Glamis Wood.
Meigle.	Rossie.

No. 1014.—Circle divided into eight segments by radial lines and each filled in with single straight-line spirals.

Ireland—
Clonmacnois (slab of Conaing M'Conghail).

No. 1015.—The same as No. 1014, but each bay filled in with double straight-line spirals finished off with black triangles.

MSS.—Gospels of MacDurnan.

No. 1016.—The same as No. 1015, but with additional bars forming circular arcs branching out at right angles from the radial bars.

MSS.—Book of Kells.

No. 1017.—Two concentric circles, the inner one like No. 1015 and the outer ring divided into eight segments, each filled in with a double straight-line spiral.

Wales—
Pen Arthur, Pembrokeshire.

No. 1018.—Circle divided into eight rhombuses filled in with double straight-line spirals, eight squares filled in with swastica straight-line spirals, and eight triangles round the circumference filled in with double straight-line spirals.

Metalwork—Saracenic Casket, 13th cent., in British Museum.

No 1019.—Tree key-pattern of same type as No. 967, adapted to fit an annular space.
The Maiden Stone.

No. 1020.—The straight border key-pattern, No. 932, adapted to fit an annular space.
Nigg.

No. 1021.—The straight border key-pattern, No. 944, modified to fit an annular space.
Tarbet, No. 6.

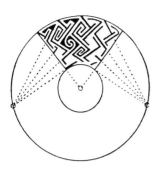

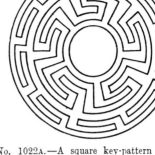

No. 1022.—The straight border key-pattern, No. 956, adapted to fit the fan-shaped segment of an annular ring, some of the square bays being filled in with double straight-line spirals and others with double curved spirals.

No. 1022A.—A square key-pattern of the Greek fret type, arranged in two concentric rings.

Hilton of Cadbol.

Basketwork [1]—Arizona coiled basket, Smithsonian Museum, Washington.

No. 1022B.—The straight border key-pattern, No. 944, adapted to fit an annular space. It differs from No. 1021 in having the white space between each of the two black triangles in the square bays in the centre facing tangentially instead of radially.

MSS.—Book of Kells.

[1] This is another instance showing how key-patterns may have had their origin in the mechanical necessities of manufacture.

ge references in italics
dicate that illustrations are on
at page, or (in the case of
our plates) facing that page.

Allen, J. Romilly, ix, x, 3, 13, 34,
    42, 61
  patterns, 1, 4, 7, 9, 11, 12, 13,
    17, 26, 27, 41, 44, 45, 47
Almouth, Northumberland,
    pattern, 45
Anglo-Saxon period, x
annular Z pattern, 54–5
arch design
  hook pattern, 57
  Z pattern, 56

Barrochan, pattern, 47
Book of Durrow, x
Book of Kells see Kells, Book of
border designs, 1, 2, 48
British Museum Bible Reg. 1.E.vi,
    pattern, 9
Burghead, Aberdeenshire,
    pattern, 13, 20, 52

Castle Dermot, Ireland, pattern,
    26
Celtic Art in Pagan and Christian
    Times (Romilly Allen), ix
Celtic Art, the Methods of
    Construction (Bain), x
Celtic Knotwork (Bain), ix, x, 2, 3
circular spirals see curved
    spirals
Clonmacnois, Ireland, pattern, 47
Collieburn stone, Caithness,
    pattern, 23
corners, 22, 48, 50
curved spirals, ix, 12

diagonal setting out, 52–61
diamond-shaped motifs, 46
Dupplin, near Forteviot, Tayside,
    pattern, 17
Durrow, Book of, x

end treatment, 17

Farr stone, Caithness, pattern, 36
finishing treatments, 1
flags, 11, 15, 40

Gattonside (near Melrose),
    pattern, 7
geometry, Celtic use of, ix, 2, 3
Golden Grove, Carmarthen,
    pattern, 47
Gospels of Macdurnan, pattern,
    45, 47
Govan, Strathclyde, No.34,
    pattern, 12
graph paper, ix, x, 1, 38, 39

half-Z pattern (V pattern), 1–2, 26
hanging branch pattern, 35, 39
Holy Island, Northumbria, x
hook patterns, ix, 33–40, 57
Hurworth, Durham, pattern, 13

Inchcolm, Fife, frontispiece
    pattern, 7
Invergowrie, Angus, 27, 42
    pattern, 28, 42
irregular shape, 53

Jedburgh, Roxburghshire, 51
Jordanhill Stone, Glasgow,
    pattern, 14, 21

Kells, Ireland, pattern, 13, 27 see
    also Kells, Book of
Kells, Book of, x
  Folio 1v, 33
    pattern, 24, 25
  Folio 2v, 48
    pattern, 11, 20
  Folio 3R, pattern, 46
  Folio 4R, pattern, 12, 32
  Folio 5R, pattern, 45
  Folio 8R, pattern, 32, 49
  Folio 18R, pattern, 12
  Folio 27v, ix
  Folio 202v, 49
    pattern, 29, 30, 31
  Folio 277v, pattern, 47
  Folio 290v, 64
    pattern, 28
  Folio 291v, 65
    pattern, 28

key patterns
  characteristics of, ix
  construction methods, x
  see also diagonal setting out;
    half-Z patterns; hook
    patterns; panel shapes,
    treatments and
    embellishments; small
    patterns; W patterns; Z
    patterns
knotwork, ix, 2

Lindisfarne, x
Lindisfarne Gospels, x
  Folio 17b, pattern, 3, *16*
  Folio 94b, pattern, 40
  Folio 95, pattern, ix, *17*, 37
  Folio 138b, pattern, 33, 36, 38
  Folio 210b, *32*, 34, 36
    pattern, 50
Llantwit Major, Llangevelach,
  Glamorganshire, pattern, 26,
  45

Macdurnan, Gospels of, pattern,
  45, 47
Margam, Glamorgan, pattern, 47
Meigle No.20, pattern, 17, 18, 19,
  22
mirrored key patterns, 1, 26, 33

Nevern, Pembrokeshire, pattern,
  45, 47
Nigg Stone, Easter Ross, pattern,
  14, 21
Norham, Northumberland,
  pattern, 13, 20

oval pattern, 58–9

panel shapes, treatments and
  embellishments, 48–51
paths as characteristic of key
  patterns, ix, 2
Pictish hook patterns, 36, 37
Picts, x, 52
plain paper, 1, 52

Rosemarkie, Easter Ross, 1
  No.1, *xi, 10*
    pattern, 12, 35, 61

S figures, internal, 15

St Andrews, Fife
  pattern, 1, 42, 45, 47
  No.10, pattern, 12, 13, 20
  No.14, *17*
    pattern, 11, 15, 20, 21, 22
St Donnans, Eigg, Inner
  Hebrides, *8*
St Vigeans, Tayside, No.12,
  pattern, 11, 16, 20
Saxons, x
semi-circular arch designs, 56,
  57
shifting direction, 49
small patterns, 41–7
spirals *see* curved spirals;
  straight-line spirals
squared paper *see* graph paper
straight-line spirals, ix, 1, 23, 24,
  25, 26, 27
  single, ix, 33
  double, ix, 11, 12, 13, 14, 21, 33
  quadruple, 17, 22
'swastika' centres, 17, 18

triangles
  characteristic of key patterns,
    ix
  and diagonal setting out, 55,
    56, 59, 60
  and half-Z patterns, 2
  and hook patterns, 33, 36, 40
  and small patterns, 41, 43, 44,
    46, 47
  and W patterns, 26, 27, 28, 29,
    30, 31
  and Z patterns, 6, 7, 9, 10, 15,
    18, 20, 21, 22, 23, 24, 55, 56,
    59, 60

V pattern, 1–2, 26

W patterns, 26–32
Wales, small patterns from, x, 41,
  47

X centres, motifs with, 45

Z patterns
  diagonal setting out, 52–6,
    58–60
  how to work, 3–10, 32
  introduction to, 1–2
  in small motifs, 43, 44, 45, 47
  with internal variations, 11–25
  mentioned, ix